SOLDIERS
OF THE CIVIL WAR

TIM ROCHE

Heinemann Library
Chicago, Illinois

www.heinemannraintree.com
Visit our website to find out more information about Heinemann-Raintree books.

To order:
☎ Phone 888-454-2279
🖳 Visit www.heinemannraintree.com to browse our catalog and order online.

©2011 Heinemann Library
an imprint of Capstone Global Library, LLC
Chicago, Illinois

Edited by Megan Cotugno
Designed by Ryan Frieson
Illustrated by Mapping Specialists, Ltd.
Picture research by Tracy Cummins
Originated by [select]
Printed in [select]

14 13 12 11 10
10 9 8 7 6 5 4 3 2 1

Library of Congress Cataloging-in-Publication Data

Roche, Tim.
    Soldiers of the Civil War / Tim Roche. — 1st ed.
      p. cm. — (Why we fought, the Civil War)
    Includes bibliographical references and index.
    ISBN 978-1-4329-3914-4 (hc)
    1. United States. Army—History—Civil War, 1861-1865—Juvenile literature. 2. Confederate States of America. Army—History—Juvenile literature. 3. United States. Army—Military life—History—19th century—Juvenile literature. 4. Confederate States of America. Army—Military life—History—19th century—Juvenile literature. 5. United States—History—Civil War, 1861-1865—Juvenile literature. 6. Soldiers—United States—History—19th century—Juvenile literature. I. Title.
    E607.R63 2001
    973.7'13—dc22
                        2009050064

Acknowledgments

The author and publishers are grateful to the following for permission to reproduce copyright material:

Corbis pp. 10, 15 (© Bettmann), 12 (© The Corcoran Gallery of Art, Washington, DC/Gift of William Wilson Corcoran); Getty Images pp. 4, 11; Library of Congress Prints and Photographs Division pp. 7, 8, 9, 13, 14, 17, 19, 20, 21, 23, 25, 29, 30, 31, 32, 33, 34, 35, 36, 39, 43; National Archives pp. 16, 27; The Art Archive p. 38 (Culver Pictures); The Granger Collection, New York pp. 24, 37, 41.

Cover photo of group of soldiers (early 1860s) reproduced with permission from Library of Congress Prints and Photographs Division.

We would like to thank Dr. James I. Robertson, Jr. for his invaluable help in the preparation of this book.

Contents

Throughout this book, you will find green text boxes that contain facts and questions to help you interact with a primary source. Use these questions as a way to think more about where our historical information comes from.

Some words are shown in bold, **like this**. You can find out what they mean by looking in the glossary, on page 46.

Why Did We Fight the Civil War?

The Civil War was a conflict between Northern states and Southern states. It was sometimes called "The War Between the States." The armies of the Union fought for the United States of America (also called the North), while the armies of the Confederacy fought for the Confederate States of America (also called the South).

Differences in Economy

The **economy** in the North was based on industry. The economy of the South was based on agriculture. In the North, people worked in factories that manufactured goods. In the South, plantations produced crops such as tobacco and cotton. In fact, the South produced three-quarters of the world's cotton. Southerners believed cotton was so important to the world that they said, "Cotton is King."

The South used slaves to work in the fields on plantations. Although some people in the South were against slavery, many more in the North opposed it. Those people who were against slavery were called **abolitionists**.

Slaves stand in front of their shack in the mid-19th century.

The Mason-Dixon Line

Though it formed part of the borders of only four states, the Mason-Dixon Line was the cultural boundary between North and South. The South, or the eleven states of the Confederacy, was sometimes called "Dixie." Some people believed the name Dixie came from the Mason-Dixon Line, but others said it came from a **banknote** in Louisiana. The area around New Orleans was called "Dixieland." Later, people called most of the states in the South "Dixie."

This map shows the division of the North and South in 1861.

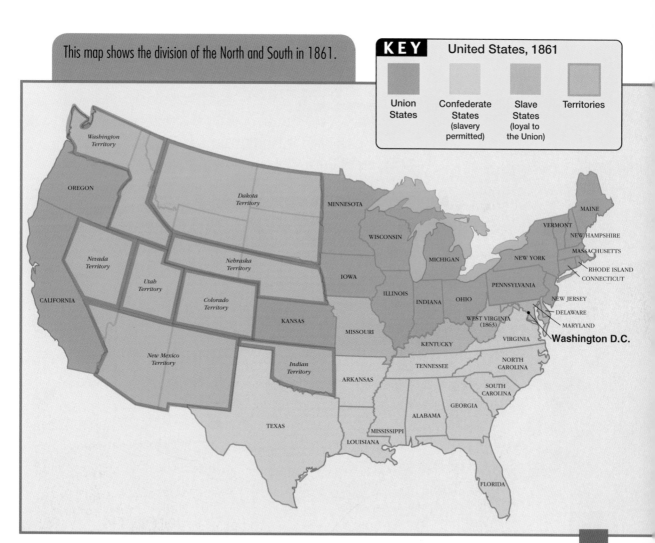

KEY United States, 1861

Union States

Confederate States (slavery permitted)

Slave States (loyal to the Union)

Territories

Why Did People Fight?

In the North the main reason men joined the fight and became soldiers was to preserve the Union, or to keep all the states together as one country. In the South they fought for **states' rights**. The idea of states' rights was that if a state, or a group of states, disagreed with the **federal** government, it always had the right to **secede** and become a separate country.

Slavery

Another reason some states wished to secede, especially those in the Deep South, was to maintain slavery. The large plantations that depended on slave labor were generally found in the southernmost states. It was not until after the fight at Fort Sumter that states in the upper South decided to secede. Some Southern soldiers did not like slavery, but fought for the Confederacy anyway because the South was their home. Some Northerners wanted slavery abolished and fought the South wanting to help make that happen.

WRITING WAR LETTERS

Civil War soldiers faced many difficulties and dangers, marching and fighting away from home and their families. Many men wrote letters home to their loved ones. The only way to communicate was through letters, and some men wrote hundreds of them over the course of the war. Thomas Halsey was a farmer from New Jersey. He volunteered for service in the late summer of 1862, and wrote many letters home to his wife "Lib."

"Camp Fort Marcy, September 5, 1862

Dear Wife,

…We have been expecting an attack from the enemy but I think the danger is passed and it may yet be some time before we have a brush with the enemy. I like soldiering full as well as I expected. It keeps my mind constantly employed and my health and appetite being good, I make out to pass the time quite pleasantly. But after all, Lib, I miss my quiet home, the prattle of my children and the companionship of a loving wife. But duty called me in the service of my country, and I feel I ought to be here…

Yours ever,"

[From *Field of Battle: The Civil War Letters of Major Thomas J. Halsey*, p. 14.]

Union soldiers are pictured here. This photo was taken in August 1862.

Who Were the Leaders?

The president of the United States of America was Abraham Lincoln. The president of the **Confederate States of America** was Jefferson Davis.

Abraham Lincoln

Before he became president, Lincoln was a lawyer in Illinois, and before that a member of the **U.S. House of Representatives**. Lincoln's greatest concern was to preserve the Union. He wanted to find a way of keeping all the states together as one country. By July of 1862, President Lincoln understood that victory would not be possible without solving the problem of slavery. He decided to end the question of whether slavery could exist in the United States by abolishing it. Lincoln abolished slavery in the Confederate states with the **Emancipation Proclamation**.

Even though some slaves had to wait until the war's end to become free, the Emancipation Proclamation sent a strong message that slavery would come to an end forever.

Abraham Lincoln was born in a one-room log cabin in Kentucky. In March 1861, he became the first U.S. president to have been born outside the thirteen colonies.

Jefferson Davis

Jefferson Davis was a **West Point** graduate and a member of the **U.S. Senate** from Mississippi. He resigned from the Senate when Mississippi seceded from the Union. He became the president of the Confederate States of America.

Primary Source: Jefferson Davis

Jefferson Davis grew up in Mississippi. He was the youngest of ten children. His father had fought in the **Revolutionary War**. He became president of the Confederacy in February 1861.

Thinking About the Source:

What is the first thing you notice about this photograph?

When do you think this photo of Davis was taken?

If this photo was taken today, what would be different?

Ulysses S. Grant

Ulysses S. Grant was the son of a tanner. He entered **West Point** at the age of 17. Grant fought in the **Mexican-American War** before Lincoln appointed him a general in the Civil War. In 1864 Lincoln made Grant commander of all U.S. armies.

WEST POINT

Many Union and Confederate officers attended the United States Military Academy at West Point. West Point is the oldest military school in the country. Students are officers-in-training and called cadets. When cadets graduate, they become **commissioned officers.**

President Lincoln liked Grant because he fought hard and won many battles.

Robert E. Lee

Robert E. Lee was also a graduate of West Point and had fought in the Mexican-American War. In 1861 President Lincoln asked Lee to be commander of Union forces, but Lee would not accept, as his home state of Virginia was **seceding**.

Lee fought for the Confederacy, and specifically his home state of Virginia. Although he had once owned slaves, he was thought to be at least somewhat against slavery. He did not want Virginia to secede from the Union in the first place. He came to see that the South's fight against the North's bigger army, and in defense of slavery, was a lost cause.

BATTLE OF THE WILDERNESS

Lee and Grant's armies did not meet on the battlefield until 1864, less than a year before the war ended, at the Battle of the Wilderness. Both sides sustained heavy **casualties**.

General Lee was much loved and respected by his men. Here he is seen on his famous horse, Traveler.

Generals Jackson and Sherman

General "Stonewall" Jackson was probably the most famous Confederate commander besides General Lee. He fought in the First Battle of Bull Run, also known as First Manassas, which was the first major battle of the Civil War. Jackson was a general at the time. His **brigade** held their ground against superior forces waiting for **reinforcements**. Because he held his ground, not moving an inch, he earned the nickname "Stonewall" and became a major general.

Jackson died in May 1863, after being accidentally shot by his own men. He had to have his left arm **amputated**, and died eight days later from complications due to pneumonia. His death was a setback in **morale** for the soldiers and for the entire South.

Union General Sherman served under General Grant, and later as commander of the Western Theater. The Western Theater was the part of the war that took place west of the Appalachian Mountains all the way to the Mississippi River. Later, it also included Sherman's armies in Georgia and the Carolinas.

Stonewall Jackson was a smart fighter and an important general to the South. He was a graduate of **West Point**.

March to the Sea

Sherman is best known for his capture of Atlanta and famous March to the Sea. After taking Atlanta, an important city in the South, Sherman began his March to the Sea. He lost touch with supply lines and resorted to searching for food. He ordered troops to destroy crops and livestock that the Union army could not take with it. He also ordered his troops to destroy factories. General Sherman and General Grant believed the Civil War would end only when the Confederates lost the will to fight.

After the Civil War, when Grant became president, Sherman succeeded him as the top U.S. general.

William Tecumseh Sherman was a famous Union general known for his capture of Atlanta and his March to the Sea. He was a graduate of West Point.

Who Were the Soldiers in the Civil War?

Most men enlisted, or volunteered, for service. Some received a commission as an officer. Later in the war, men were also **drafted**.

Men who received a commission were typically educated at a military academy such as West Point. They held a higher rank than most volunteers and were usually appointed by their state's governor or the president. Although a great many volunteer soldiers fought bravely, only a few received the fame in battle that some **commissioned officers** received.

Cavalrymen

Cavalrymen fought battles on horseback, though some rode to battle and then fought on foot. **Cavalry** units were important because they were so mobile. The swift tactics used by cavalry were often disruptive to the enemy. Cavalry units were most effective for long-distance raids and gathering intelligence about the enemy.

Cavalry could make a big difference in a war in the 1800s.

Infantry Soldiers

Infantry soldiers were the backbone of the army. They fought on foot and walked from place to place carrying their rifles and **bayonets**. Men also carried their **rations** in **haversacks**.

Soldiers assigned to field **artillery** were responsible for firing cannons. Because of the weight, soldiers required horses to pull the trailers that carried the cannons.

Primary Source: Union Army Soldier

This is a photograph of Union Army Private W.C. Arnold.

Thinking About the Source:

What objects are shown in the photograph?

What is the physical setting?

What other details can you see?

Other Notable Soldiers

James Ewell Brown Stuart, known as Jeb, was a famous Confederate **cavalry** commander. He attended **West Point** and was in the **federal** army, but resigned before his state **seceded**. He was shot and killed on May 11, 1864.

What Was the Mystery of Special Orders 191?

In late summer 1862, soon after the Confederate army invaded Maryland, a group of Union soldiers from the 27th Indiana Infantry found a copy of General Lee's Special Orders number 191. They found the special orders in a field, wrapped around three cigars. How they came to be there is unknown. Who may have dropped them and to whom they were being delivered is also not precisely known.

Finding the orders turned out to be very important. They described how General Lee's army was split into two. The Union saw this as an opportunity to attack a weakened Confederate army.

Stuart was known to wear a cape with red lining and a hat with a peacock feather. Because of this, some of the soldiers called him "Beauty."

The Battle of Antietam

Four days later the Union army attacked. The Battle of Antietam began. It was the first battle on Northern soil. It was the bloodiest day in American history. On the Confederate side, Generals Lee, Jackson, and Longstreet commanded. The Union generals were McClellan, Hooker, Sumner, and Burnside.

Both sides suffered high **casualties**, but Antietam was a strategic victory for the Union, because it forced General Lee's army back into the South. It also gave President Lincoln the victory he needed to announce his **Emancipation Proclamation**.

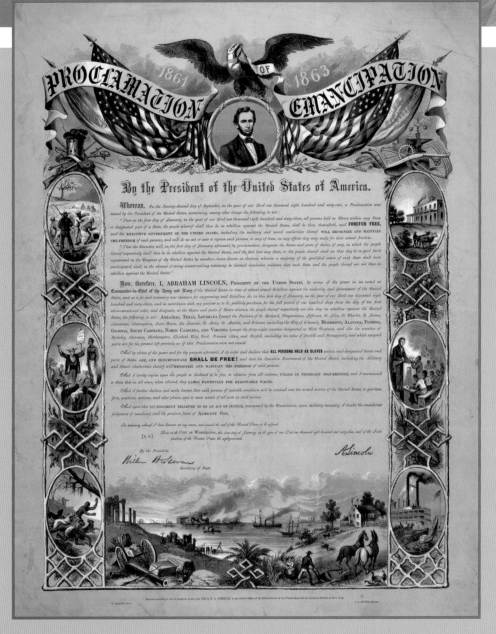

Primary Source:
Emancipation Proclamation

Abraham Lincoln announced the Emancipation Proclamation shortly after Antietam. It represented a shift in war strategy. No longer was the war only about preserving the Union; it was now also about the abolition of slavery.

Thinking About the Source:

Describe the details that you see in the image.

Why do you think these particular details were chosen for this printing of the Emancipation Proclamation?

What Was Life Like as a Soldier?

Life as a soldier was demanding. Confederate soldiers often had it worse than Union soldiers because they were not as well supplied. A soldier literally risked life and limb. At the time of the Civil War, many wounded arms and legs could not be saved. Doctors would **amputate** them. In battles with many wounded soldiers, limbs would be thrown into piles.

Risky Surgeries

Bullets traveled more slowly then and tended to do great damage. Surgeons often used their fingers to probe for them. If a soldier had any **anesthesia**, it was likely to be chloroform, which was used to put him to sleep during surgery. Ether was also used occasionally, as was morphine. If all else failed, sometimes whiskey or brandy was available. If a soldier survived an operation, he still had to worry about infection. Since hospitals were out in the fields, they were not very clean. Only about one out of three soldiers who died in the Civil War actually died in battle.

WAR LETTERS

"My Own darling Mother I reckon you all feel a little uneasiness not having heard from me for so long. I have been sick in the hospital since Tuesday morning. Dr. says I am improving. I have had an attack bilious fever am so weak that it has been quite an effort for me to write this much but knowing that you would be uneasy I thought I would try write this much. The boy comes to take it to the office. I remain your attached son Kent"

[From *The Valley of the Shadow Personal Papers*—Augusta County: Jacob Kent Langhorne to His Mother, October 20, 1862.]

Primary Source:
Confederate Wounded, 1862

Doctors were in great demand during the war. They did their best to attend wounded soldiers between battles. Here, soldiers in the 14th Indiana **Infantry** are treated after the Battle of Antietam.

Thinking About the Source:

What is the physical setting of this photograph?

Think about hospitals and medicine now. What would be different if this photograph were taken today?

Is there anything else you notice in this image?

Supplies for the Soldiers

Soldiers often faced disruptions in their supply lines. This meant they did not get enough to eat. They would sometimes have to find food themselves. Many soldiers could not find clean food and water. Some of them caught **dysentery** and often died from it. When a soldier did receive **rations**, they were usually salted pork, preserved beef, **hardtack**, and coffee. Fresh vegetables were hard to find, and fresh fruit was rare.

WAR LETTERS

December 28, 1863 Camp Near Stephensville, Virginia

"Dear Father and Step Mother— …Thanks be to God, my soule shall be fed with Heavenly Food. Than I am satisfied with a few hard tack and cold water. We have more than that. This is our rations for a day but it does not satisfy my appetite. Now, this day's ration for one man-ten hard tack-1 1/2 pound beef-3 tablespoons of coffee and about 3 tablespoons of sugar. Then we have a change sometimes. We draw 2 potatoes-2 onions-a few beans-a small portion of rice and then a portion of pork. We do not get this all in one day. This is a change. Then we get a small loaf of bread. The first I mentioned is a days rations. They say it will be plenty after awhile. But I can't see the point…
F. Rosenbery"

[From *The Valley of the Shadow Personal Papers*—Franklin County: Franklin Rosenbery to John Abraham Rosenbery (father) and probably Mary Jane Snider (stepmother).]

Women often helped tend to the wounded in camp. Here, a woman and her three children stand next to a soldier (possibly her husband) in a camp near Washington, D.C.

Clara Barton was a nurse during the Civil War.

"ANGELS OF THE BATTLEFIELD"

Two thousand women volunteered as nurses in the Civil War. They tended many soldiers. The famous author Louisa May Alcott was one of many volunteers who wrote about her experience as a Civil War nurse. Clara Barton was also a Civil War nurse.

What Was the Turning Point in the Civil War?

There were several possible turning points in the Civil War. In the spring of 1863, General Lee led his men in a second invasion of the North. He hoped to be successful in battle and convince President Lincoln to give up fighting the war.

Then, in July, two major battles occurred. One was in the west and one was in the east. Before the Battle of Vicksburg and the Battle of Gettysburg, the Confederacy was probably at its greatest strength. After these two losses, the Confederates were never again the same.

The Battle of Gettysburg

The Battle of Gettysburg had the greatest number of **casualties** of any battle of the Civil War. Gettysburg was Lee's second failed attempt to fight in the North. After that, he never again tried to invade.

A key **tactical** action at Gettysburg was the Union defense of Little Round Top, ending with a **bayonet** charge led by Colonel Joshua Lawrence Chamberlain. Had Chamberlain been unsuccessful in protecting Little Round Top, Cemetery Ridge would have been vulnerable to Confederate attack. The Union would have had to abandon that strategic position, and the North might not have won Gettysburg. Chamberlain was wounded in battle but received life-long fame because of his bravery.

Primary Source: Battle of Gettysburg

The Battle of Gettysburg was a Union victory at great cost to both sides.

In the above photograph, Union soldiers lie dead on the field after the bloody battle.

Thinking About the Source:

Does this photograph change any opinion that you had of the Civil War?

Why do you think this photograph was taken?

Compare this photo with an image of the Battle of Gettysburg taking place. Do the two images inspire the same emotions in you?

Cemetery Ridge and Pickett's Charge

The day after the fight on Little Round Top, General Lee ordered Confederate General George Pickett to attack at Cemetery Ridge. This was a bad idea, since the Union still held Little Round Top. The Confederacy failed to break through the Union's line and suffered heavy losses.

> **GENERAL GEORGE PICKETT**
>
> General George Pickett was another soldier educated at **West Point**. He graduated last in his class of 59 cadets.

Pickett's men make their charge on the Union soldiers on July 3, 1863 in Cemetery Ridge.

The Gettysburg Address

Four months after the Battle of Gettysburg, President Lincoln gave a speech for the dedication of Soldiers' National Cemetery in Gettysburg. Though it came after the **Emancipation Proclamation**, the Gettysburg Address helped redefine the war as not just a struggle for the Union, but as a struggle for universal freedom.

"...and that government: of the people, by the people, for the people, shall not perish from the earth."
—Lincoln's Gettysburg Address

THE GETTYSBURG ADDRESS

The Gettysburg Address, though rather short, is one of Abraham Lincoln's most famous speeches. It was not even the main speech of the day, but it has gone down as one of the greatest in American history.

What Role Did the Navy Play in the War?

Both the Union and the Confederacy had navies. Most ships were made of wood, but some were protected by iron or steel plates. These were called ironclads. Ironclads were steam powered. Ironclads made a big impact when they first fought in battle. Shells from other gunboats bounced off their armor. The South was the first to use an ironclad, but before long the North had many more in service. The North had the advantage of having more factories to build ships.

> ### BATTLE BETWEEN IRONCLADS
> The first battle between ironclads was in 1862. The CSS *Virginia* of the South fought the USS *Monitor* of the North.

Admiral Farragut

Union Admiral David Glasgow Farragut was the Civil War's most famous naval officer. The Battle of Mobile Bay was his biggest triumph. It was strategically important. During battle, Farragut climbed to the top of his ship, the *Hartford*, and tied himself to the mast, as an inspiration to the other sailors. When another ship in his fleet, the Tecumseh, hit a **torpedo**, Farragut was said to have shouted, "Full speed ahead!"

Robert Smalls

Robert Smalls was a slave aboard a boat in the harbor in Charleston, South Carolina. Left alone one night, he stole the boat and headed north. Not only did Smalls help his family to escape, he also helped the families of several other African-American crewmen. Additionally, there was **artillery** and a codebook of secret Confederate signals on board.

Lincoln rewarded Smalls and his crew for their bravery with prize money, and they became famous throughout the North. A few months later, in August 1862, Smalls met with the president a second time and persuaded him to allow African Americans to fight for the Union. Smalls became a pilot for the Union navy. After the war, he entered politics and served in the **U.S. House of Representatives**.

ADMIRAL DAVID GLASGOW FARRAGUT

Union officer David Glasgow Farragut was the first rear admiral, vice admiral, and full admiral of the navy. He joined the navy when he was only ten years old. He is one of only six naval officers to be bestowed the honor of serving on active duty for life. During the Battle of Mobile Bay, Farragut fought against Admiral Franklin Buchanan, commander of the Southern fleet.

Both the North and South had navies, but the North was able to build more ships more quickly with its supplies and factories.

What Were Deserters?

Desertion became a problem for both sides later in the war. Hundreds of thousands fled the battlefield. In the summer of 1862, soldiers began to leave the army in large numbers due to low **morale**. It was against the law for them to leave the war. States were unable to meet their **quotas** and began to conscript, or **draft**, men. Lincoln said deserters outnumbered new **recruits**.

The Draft Act

The Federal Draft Act in March 1863 was unpopular. Draftees could pay $300 for a substitute. In the end, the draftees made up only a very small percentage of Union soldiers. Southerners for a time could hire substitutes, too. States and counties paid bounties (money) to encourage men to volunteer. The **federal** government contributed part of the bounty. Bounties reached $1,000 by late in the war. Some men would enlist, get their bounty, desert, and reenlist in a different location.

Desertion

Later in the war, desertion was common among volunteers. This was especially true in the South, where many were boys of just 14–17 years. Men deserted not just for fear of being wounded in battle, but also due to food shortage and disease. Punishments for deserters who were caught grew severe. Some soldiers were imprisoned, whipped, or shot. For many, only a presidential pardon (forgiveness for a crime) could save them. Rather than face the **stockade**, some soldiers just switched sides.

WAR LETTERS

Camp near Beverly Ford, Virginia

September 13, 1863 "Dear Wife, ...I have not got my Commission yet as Major and I may not get it. I shall not fret over it.... There are to be two men shot next Friday for Desertion. One of them from our Regiment. We shall have to go & see the execution. It will be a sad sight.... It is hard enough to see men shot on the battlefield. Oh what a horrible thing war is. I shall be a happy man when it is over, if I live to see it. I had a letter from Mr. Thompson. He informed me that Mrs. Condicts baby was sick and that there was quite a good deal of sickness about the neighborhood. I hope our dear little ones may keep well as well as yourself. Your affectionate and loveing husband,"

[From *Field of Battle: The Civil War Letters of Major Thomas J. Halsey*, p. 92.]

Primary Source: Civil War Substitutes

Those who could afford it could pay for a substitute and avoid fighting.

The below print was a wood engraving done in 1862. It is a scene between a wealthy Fifth Avenue (New York) couple.

Thinking About the Source:

What do you notice first about the image?

What people and objects are shown?

What, if any, words can you read?

SCENE, FIFTH AVENUE.

HE. "Ah! Dearest ADDIE! I've succeeded. I've got a Substitute!"
SHE. "Have you? What a curious coincidence! And *I* have found one FOR YOU!"

Brother Against Brother

Even though Confederate and Union soldiers fought against each other, many did not feel angry toward the enemy. Sometimes **picket lines** from either army would shout at each other from a distance to establish a "peace zone" and avoid fighting. Many volunteer soldiers fought in places on the border between North and South. Some families had a brother who fought for the North, and another who fought for the South.

Occasionally, soldiers would swap **provisions** with soldiers on the other side. For instance, if one had cornmeal but no coffee and the other coffee but no cornmeal, a deal to swap could be made.

Fighting in the Civil War sometimes meant battling against family or friends. Below, the Confederate and Union soldiers meet in the bloody battle of Atlanta.

In the Civil War prison camp pictured, Union soldiers are guarding Confederate prisoners. Soldiers tried hard to avoid capture. If captured by the enemy, they would be sent to a military prison. Conditions in many prisons were terrible, and captured soldiers were not fed very well. In many prisons, such as Andersonville, Georgia, and Elmira, New York, large numbers of soldiers died of starvation.

Who Else Fought in the Civil War?

The Zouaves were volunteers who dressed in colorful outfits modeled after the French army **infantry**. In the 1800s, many other countries had French-inspired Zouave regiments. The Union had almost three times as many Zouave units as the Confederacy.

Zouaves typically wore baggy pants, a sash, a short jacket, and sometimes even a fez (round cap) with a colorful tassel.

Women in the War

Many women served in both armies as nurses and general helpers. They marched to battles with the men, bandaging and sheltering the wounded. Less well known is the fact that a number of women disguised themselves as men in order to fight as soldiers. These women had various reasons for serving. Some wanted to fight alongside their husbands. Some sought to escape a bad home life, arranged marriages, or even their home countries across the sea. Most of them served bravely, and some even received retirement money after the war. Some of them suffered illness and injury, and then were discharged (kicked out of the military) before the end of the war when found out to be women.

LORETA JANETA VELAZQUEZ

One interesting woman who worked as a female spy and fought as a male soldier was Loreta Janeta Velazquez. She was born in Cuba and claimed in her book, *The Woman in Battle*, to have fought for the Confederate army as Henry Buford.

Many Civil War soldiers fought in **brigades** of their own nationality. Meagher's Irish Brigade and the Italian Garibaldi Guard are two famous examples. Germans, Swedes, Jews, Austrians, and many others fought as well.

African-American Soldiers

Around 185,000 African-American soldiers fought in the Union army. Half were freedmen living in the North, and half were former slaves from the South, some of whom had escaped to freedom.

African Americans not only fought bravely in the Civil War, but a regiment of freedmen fought alongside George Washington in the **Revolutionary War** as well.

SARAH EMMA EDMONDS

Sarah Emma Edmonds served in the 2nd Michigan Infantry as Frank Thompson. For a time she worked as a spy, disguising herself as an African-American man and later as an Irish woman named Bridget O'Shea. When she contracted **malaria**, she checked into a private hospital to avoid being found out as a woman. But the army thought "Frank Thompson" was a deserter. Rather than face the firing squad, she went to Washington, DC, to serve as a female nurse.

African-American soldiers fought bravely for the Union, risking death or slavery if captured.

Irregular Soldiers

Irregulars were citizen soldiers who operated behind enemy lines. They were not part of the regular army, though leaders of these fighters kept in touch with the army. Irregulars would often destroy bridges and generally make life difficult for the enemy. The Confederacy produced the most famous irregular leaders.

Mosby's Rangers

The 43rd Virginia **Cavalry** Battalion was a group of Confederate soldiers who fought on horseback. The group was also known as "Mosby's Rangers." Because Mosby's Rangers were irregulars, they could act more quickly than regular troops. Mosby often led his men on raids without telling them their objective until they arrived.

Mosby and his men often lived in the farmhouses of **sympathizers**. They had no **base camp** and could disappear like ghosts. Often operating deep in Union territory, Mosby's Rangers were responsible for disrupting supply lines. A few weeks after Lee surrendered, Mosby disbanded his men, refusing to surrender formally.

JOHN MOSBY

John Mosby was known as the "Gray Ghost" because he could hit a target quickly and depart without a trace. He was said to have bright blue eyes and an iron will. Mosby attacked by both day and night, but preferred to work in the dark of night.

The 43rd Virginia Cavalry Battalion was formed in June 1863. Not long after it was formed, John Mosby took over command, and it became better known as Mosby's Rangers.

Many people consider Nathan Bedford Forrest the greatest cavalry leader of the Civil War. He and his men were part of the regular cavalry. Because they operated deep behind enemy lines, they were considered "irregular" in nature. Forrest's nickname was "The Wizard of the Saddle." He was one of very few soldiers on either side to start as a **private** and end the war as a general. He and his men fought in the Western Theater of the war.

Who Were the Civil War Artists?

There were many people who contributed to the war effort through their art. Some of them fought in battle, and some did not.

Musicians

Music was important to soldiers in the Civil War. Music helped keep up **morale**. Both the Confederate and Union armies had bands that traveled in **regiments**. By the end of 1861, about one in 40 soldiers was a musician.

"DIXIE"

One of the most popular Confederate songs was "Dixie." President Lincoln was fond of the song. At a rally near the end of the war he asked to have it played. He said, "That tune is now Federal property . . . good to show the rebels that, with us in power, they will be free to hear it again."

Walt Whitman

Primary Source: Walt Whitman

Walt Whitman was a famous poet who worked as a volunteer nurse and a clerk during the war. Whitman's poem "O Captain My Captain" was written for Abraham Lincoln.

Thinking About the Source:

When do you think this photograph was taken?

If someone took this photo today, what would be different? Would anything be the same?

Ambrose Bierce was a famous journalist and short-story writer who fought in the Battle of Shiloh. He wrote the famous story "An Occurrence at Owl Creek Bridge."

On the battlefield musicians played bugles, drums, and fifes. Sometimes they played whole songs, but the musicians did much more than that. Buglers were responsible for knowing how to play many different calls. These calls let soldiers know what to do on the battlefield or when it was time for a meal. The drummers helped soldiers keep in time while marching. In the Union the drummers wore white straps to hold up their drums.

Many musicians were kids, because full-grown men were needed for fighting. When the fighting was especially fierce and many men were wounded, musicians would sometimes help doctors perform **amputations**. Music was considered so important that General Lee once said, "I don't think we could have an army without music."

At Camp

At camp some of the men played music to pass the time. Often these were not official army musicians. They were soldiers who brought their instruments from home. They played guitars, banjos, and fiddles.

Occasionally Confederate and Union forces camped across a river from one another. It was not uncommon for them to have musical duels, with soldiers on each side playing their patriotic songs. One song, "When Johnny Comes Marching Home," written in 1863, was popular with both sides. Another, "Home, Sweet Home," was also popular with both armies. A couple of times during the war, Confederate and Union soldiers even played and sang the song together, from across a river!

Harriet Beecher Stowe was an author and **abolitionist**. She wrote the widely talked about antislavery novel *Uncle Tom's Cabin*. The book was the best-selling novel of the 1800s and was very influential. President Lincoln, on meeting Stowe, is quoted as saying, "So this is the little woman who made this big war."

JOHN CLEM

When John Clem was nine years old he ran away from home to join the Union army. After being turned down by one unit, he was taken up by another as a drummer boy and mascot. Some of the men got a collection together to pay Clem regular wages. Two years later he was allowed to join his **regiment** properly. With his shortened **musket**, Clem once shot a Confederate colonel. After that he was promoted and became the youngest **non-commissioned officer** in U.S. army history. Clem was later photographed by Mathew Brady. He was the last Civil War veteran on duty when he officially retired in 1916.

Drummer boys called out marching orders with different beats and helped soldiers keep time.

How Did the Civil War End?

On the morning of April 9, 1865, General Lee made his last stand. The final battle occurred at Appomattox Court House. On realizing Grant's forces outmatched his own, Lee knew he had to surrender.

Terms of Surrender

Grant and Lee met that afternoon in a home owned by Wilmer McLean. They agreed on the terms of the surrender. Three days later on April 12, the Confederate army would formally surrender. Lee asked Grant if his men could keep their horses, as they would be needed at home. Grant might have worried the Confederate men would take to the hills to continue the fight using **guerrilla warfare**. Lee asked his men to go home instead. Grant generously allowed Lee's men to keep their horses and mules, and he allowed the Confederate officers to keep their **sidearms** as well.

Union officer Joshua Chamberlain, now a general, was selected to lead the formal ceremony. An order was given. The Union soldiers gave the marching salute to the Confederates, who responded with the same salute. In victory, the Union soldiers showed the Confederate soldiers honor and respect.

The Confederate soldiers passed by and laid down their guns.

APPOMATTOX COURT HOUSE

Appomattox Court House is considered historically important. The original courthouse burned down in a fire in 1892. A new courthouse was built 4.8 kilometers (3 miles) away. The original site, including the McLean home where Grant and Lee met, is now a national historical park.

Grant (seated right) and Lee (seated left) agreed to honorable terms of surrender for the Confederates at Appomattox.

Reconstruction

It was important to President Lincoln that General Grant be generous with the rebels. President Lincoln knew that putting the country back together would not be easy. He wanted the soldiers and the country to put away any hard feelings. Grant and his Union soldiers did a good job with their respectful treatment of the Confederates.

After General Lee met General Grant, there were Confederates in other parts of the country yet to surrender. However, the war was effectively over. The era of Reconstruction would now begin.

The period of Reconstruction directly followed the Civil War. It lasted until 1877, and some of its policies were actually put in place before the war ended. The purpose of Reconstruction was to figure out how to bring the Confederate states back into the Union. Also of concern was how to treat former Confederate leaders.

WAR LETTERS

May 18, 1865

Appomattox Station, Virginia

"Dear Parents

...Forage is very scarce we only get about five quarts of oats a day and no hay and for grazing there is no grass. I don't see how the people keeps their stock... there will be any amount of Peaches in this country. this is a dull place we cannot get any papers nor any thing else when you write... I must close for this time write soon

your son

J Milton Crawford

[From *The Valley of the Shadow Personal Papers*—Franklin County: J. Milton Crawford to his Parents, May 18, 1865.]

Important Amendments

The civil rights of former slaves was an important concern during Reconstruction. The 13th, 14th, and 15th Amendments to the Constitution grew out of Reconstruction. The 13th Amendment outlawed slavery. The 14th Amendment guaranteed citizenship to former slaves and included an important section called the "Equal Protection Clause." This clause required states to provide equal protection to all people within their boundaries. The 15th Amendment said that every citizen was guaranteed the right to vote and could not be discriminated against based on "race, color or previous condition of servitude." In other words, former slaves now had the right to vote.

Primary Source:
Ruins of Richmond, Virginia

Many cities were destroyed during the Civil War and had to rebuild during the Reconstruction era.

This is a photograph of the destroyed Richmond & Petersburg Railroad Depot. The photo was taken in April 1865.

Thinking About the Source:

What do you notice first in the photo?

What people and objects are shown?

What can you learn from examining this image?

Timeline

November 1860	Abraham Lincoln is elected the 16th president of the United States.
December 1860	South Carolina secedes from the Union.
April 1861	Confederate forces fire upon Fort Sumter. States of the upper South join the deep South in secession. Lee resigns from the U.S. army and joins the Confederate army. The Civil War begins.
March 1862	CSS *Virginia* battles the USS *Monitor* in the first battle of ironclad warships.
September 1862	A copy of Lee's Special Orders 191 goes missing. A few days later the Battle of Antietam begins. It is the bloodiest single day of the war.
September 1862	President Lincoln announces his Emancipation Proclamation, taking effect January 1, 1863, and committing the Union to ending slavery forever.
January 1, 1863	Emancipation Proclamation frees slaves in Confederate states.
March 1863	Union's First Conscription Act. All men ages 20 to 45 can be called for service. While wealthier citizens might buy a substitute, the poor cannot afford it. Many protest the unfairness.
May 1863	Stonewall Jackson is accidentally shot by his own troops. He dies a few days later.
July 1863	The Battles of Gettysburg and Vicksburg take place. The Union turns back Lee's second attempt to invade the North and gains control of the Mississippi River. Many historians consider this the turning point of the war.

November 1863	President Lincoln gives his Gettysburg Address, which is considered one of the greatest speeches in American history.
August 1864	Battle of Mobile Bay takes place. Admiral Farragut's victory ends Confederate control of the last important port east of the Mississippi River.
Fall 1864	Sherman captures Atlanta and then completes his March to the Sea.
April 1865	Lee surrenders to Grant at Appomattox. The Civil War ends.
1868	Grant is elected the 18th president of the United States.

Glossary

abolitionist during the Civil War period, a person who wanted to end slavery in the United States

amputate remove a limb in a medical procedure

anesthesia medicine used to dull pain

artillery weapons, like cannons, used to fire at far-away targets

banknote federal or Confederate dollar bill

base camp fixed camp; irregulars did not have a fixed camp, but stayed in a new location almost every night

bayonet steel knife attached to the end of a rifle that is used in hand-to-hand combat

brigade large unit of ground troops

casualties losses in a battle, including the number of soldiers wounded, killed, or missing

cavalry soldiers who fight on horseback

commissioned officer position of authority in the military; commissioned officers are the commanding officers of military units

desertion leaving service as a soldier without permission, usually to return home

draft also called conscripted; being required to serve in the military

dysentery infection in the lower intestine, which is often deadly, caused by bacteria in water or food

economy system of economic activity, including commerce for producing, selling, and buying goods and services

Emancipation Proclamation document issued by President Lincoln that granted freedom to slaves living in Confederate states when those states did not return to the Union by January 1, 1863

federal related to a national government

guerrilla warfare style of combat where small groups attack and then escape, rather than facing the enemy in open battle

hardtack hard, dry cracker eaten by soldiers

haversack bag carried over the shoulder having a single strap, used to carry provisions and personal items

infantry soldiers who fight on foot, typically using rifles

malaria common disease in hot countries that people get from mosquitoes

Mexican-American War conflict between the United States and Mexico from 1846 to 1848

morale state of the soldiers' cheerfulness, discipline, and confidence

musket older long gun used by some soldiers, which was not as accurate as a rifle

non-commissioned officer lower-ranked officer; enlisted soldier holding some authority, usually obtained by being promoted

picket line soldiers whose job was to guard the outer edges of their army

private lowest rank in the army

provisions any food a soldier might find to eat, including rations, as well as other items a soldier wanted, such as tobacco and paper

quota number of new recruits each state was responsible to provide for the war

rations soldiers' food provided by the military

recruit newly enlisted or drafted member of the military

regiment military unit of up to 1,000 foot soldiers

reinforcements additional troops that come to support an army

Revolutionary War war against the British for American independence, fought 1775–1783

secede break away from something

sidearm handgun or sword worn around the waist by officers

states' rights rights and powers the states possess in relation to the federal government, as guaranteed by the Constitution

stockade jail in an army camp for that army's own soldiers

sympathizer person who helped soldiers of one side, usually Confederates, with provisions or information regarding an enemy's location

tactical referring to specific actions taken to gain advantage on the battlefield

torpedo underwater mine used to blow up enemy ships

U.S. House of Representatives lower body of the law-making branch (Congress) of the U.S. government

U.S. Senate upper body of lawmakers of the U.S. government, which has fewer members who serve longer terms than members of the House of Representatives

West Point United States military academy located at West Point, New York; many Civil War generals, North and South, attended West Point

Find Out More

Books

Abnett, Dan. *The Battle of Gettysburg*. New York: Rosen Publishing, 2007.

Flanagan, Alison K. *Women of the Union*. Mankato, MN: Compass Point Books, 2007.

Websites

www.kids.gov
This is a great site for Civil War information and all sorts of other interesting topics.

www.gettysburgfoundation.org
This website deals with all things related to Gettysburg.

DVDs

Burns, Ken. *The Civil War*. PBS DVD Video, 2004.
When this 11-hour miniseries came out in 1990, it was the most successful in television history. Called epic and a masterpiece, this documentary brings the Civil War to life.

***Secrets of the Civil War*. History Channel DVDs, 2008.**
This compilation of nine programs from the History Channel covers many lesser-known or forgotten incidents of the Civil War.

Index